PASSIONATE WORSHIP

Unveiling the Advantage of
Unconventional Worship

Passionate Worship

Unveiling the Advantage of Unconventional Worship

Copyright © 2020 by **Kayode Fagbe Daniels**

Paperback ISBN: 978-1-952098-33-8

Printed in the United States of America. All rights reserved solely by the publisher. This book or parts thereof may not be reproduced in any form, stored in a retrieval system, or transmitted in any form by any means - electronic, mechanical, photocopy. Unless otherwise noted, Bible quotations are taken from the Holy Bible, King James Version. Copyright 1982 by Thomas Nelson, Inc., publishers. Used by permission.

Published by:
Cornerstone Publishing
A Division of Cornerstone Creativity Group LLC
Info@thecornerstonepublishers.com
www.thecornerstonepublishers.com
+1 516.547.4999

Author's Contact
For speaking engagement or to order books by Pastor Kay please send email to kayodemcdaniels@gmail.com or call +1 (925) 378-8342.

PRAISES FOR PASSIONATE WORSHIP

What elevates our worship to the realm where it pleases God is passion. It is passion that separates true worship from religion and causes it to gain God's attention. This book sets out the elements of infusing our worship with passion in a very simple, direct and relatable way.

Pastor Yinka Somotun
Zonal Pastor RCCGNAO CA2 & APICP

Just as the author emphasized, Passion pursues, Passion pushes. Therefore, passionate worshippers cry out for more. More of God and less of man. It takes a true worshipper who has encountered/experienced God to pen down these useful tips for effective worship lifestyle and for worship leading. And only those who have been there can lead people to His presence.

Evangelist Toun Soetan
Trinity World Evangelical Ministries

Passionate worship elucidates why we need to engage in praise to The LORD and worship of GOD more in our generation. The points raised by the author strikes straight to the heart of the matter, praise and worship should not be an accompanying act during church meetings, but a time when the glory and power of GOD should be felt by all.

Pastor Temitope Samson
BOVAS & Company Limited

ENDORSEMENT

It is an honor and a rear privilege for me to write a recommendation about this book and the author. The book "Passionate worship" is a book that was written with passion because the author is a man full of passion. Anything that will have a lasting impact on humanity must be done with passion. A life without passion is a boring life. God want us to serve Him and worship Him in Spirit and in Truth with Passion. Therefore, worship that lacks passion is worship without focus and intentionality.

Passionate Worship is a book that will rekindle your fire for a true, intimate, and passionate worship of God. You will find in this book how to worship God passionately, the benefits of a passionate worship and how to sustain the fire of worship in your soul.

I highly recommend this book because it is loaded with divine insight, wisdom and revelation for those that want to take their worship to a whole new dimension with impact.

Kayode Fagbe Daniels, the author of this book is a Practitioner of what he wrote in this book. Kay is a man full of Passion. He is a Passionate Worshiper and a Passionate Prayer Champion.

No wonder this book is full of passionate and insightful chapters.

I have had a first hand encounter and experience of the anointing and unction upon Kayode Daniels as he prays and worships God passionately during many of our church services and on many other platforms. He is loaded with high energy and True Passion for God and His Kingdom.

Kayode wrote this book from a personal experience of his daily life of intimate and passionate worship and prayer. This book will transform, and revolutionize your worship life into Joyful daily experience.

I personally recommend this powerful book for all and sundries.

Shalom!

Yemi Oyinkansola
Lead Pastor
RCCG Jesus House Antioch, California

FOREWORD

The book "Passionate Worship" by Pastor Kayode Daniels is a masterpiece on worship for those that care to obtain knowledge about worship. Worship is a lifestyle and it can only be done in spirit and truth; anything outside spirituality and truthfulness is nothing but noise.

Neatly broken into seven chapters covering different aspects like Igniting your passion for God's presence, the ingredients of passionate worship, worship in spirit and truth, the secret of focused and undistracted worship, the secret place, the power of corporate worship and the potent weapon of warfare.

I recommend this book for all believers and lovers of kingdom projects . It is a refreshing departure from most resources out there with high spiritual content and message. Written in simple and clear language, comprehension, and understanding, small and compact to read within an hour, this book will definitely not be a problem for an average but enthusiastic reader. Happy reading.

Shalom

Pastor Ezekiel Leke Ojo
Lead Pastor, RCCG Solid Rock Phoenix Arizona.

DEDICATION

It is my utmost joy to dedicate this book to my grandfather, Pastor D. Daniels Fagbe (1904 – 2001). As a little boy, I watched him practicing covenant walk. Thank you, grandpa, for the divine generational covenant you made with the Lord and for the covenant practices you exemplified. Yes, you joined the cloud of witnesses, but you left seeds on the altar to continually offer sacrifices of worship unto the Lord Most High.

ACKNOWLEDGMENTS

I want to profoundly appreciate my sweetheart, Seun, for your support, patience and understanding while writing this book. And thanks to our first talented seed, Oluwatojuba Faith, for helping to coordinate her younger ones whenever absolute focus was required.

Certainly, this vision would not have been birthed without the "midwives" - Pastor Yemi Oyinkansola and his wife. I am deeply grateful for the push and encouragement to publish this book, as well as the mentoring. Thank you, Daddy, for truly enhancing our visions and giving us platforms to manifest God's grace upon our lives.

I am privileged to serve God among the best people on earth. Special thanks to all JHA members across the world. We love you guys dearly.

Special gratitude to Pastor Ezekiel Leke Ojo. Thank you so much for your kind heart and believing in us even when you've not met any of us.

I am also grateful to Professor (Rev) Michael & Dr. Noja Uadiale. Thank you so much for your genuine love. I acknowledge Pastor Yinka and Funke Somotun. Thank you for believing and accepting the grace we carry. Our friend, Pastor Bessie Scoggins, thank you so much.

Just like the eaglet, I have learned to fly and soar in the eye of the storm and I thank God for the mother eagle, Evangelist Toun Soetan, for the constant ministerial covering, training, mentorship, prayers, and prophetic words. Special thanks to Rev. Samson Ajetomobi of the Men of Issachar Vision.

I sincerely acknowledge Pastor Segun Olanrewaju for the leadership and mentorship. I also appreciate Pastor Temitope Samson, for your encouragement, motivation, and support.

Specials thanks to Pastor Tayo Balogun, Uncle Kola Fabiyi, Pastor Gbenga Akosh, Professor Debo Adeyewa. All of you made unforgettable impacts in my life, and groomed me to become the man I am today.

My profound gratitude goes to my mother, Mrs Bolaji Dorcas, and of course my siblings, Sis. Victoria, Pastor Biyi Daniels, Ola and Dare Daniels, for your love and prayers. I celebrate you all.

CONTENTS

Endorsement..7
Foreword..9
Dedication..11
Acknowledgments..12
Introduction...17

Chapter One
Igniting Your Passion For God's Presence....................21

Chapter Two
Ingredients of Passionate Worship................................33

Chapter Three
Worshiping in Spirit and in Truth.................................47

Chapter Four
Principles of Undistracted Worship..............................59

Chapter Five
The Secret Place..69

Chapter Six
The Power of Corporate Worship..................................79

Chapter Seven
The Potent Weapon of Warfare.................................87

About The Author..99

INTRODUCTION

My soul is filled with joy and gladness to see the birth of this work and I return all glory to God. *Passionate Worship* is a dream I had nurtured for several years and behold the realization of my dream!

One of the goals of this book is to unveil the mysteries and benefits of engaging in unconventional worship (publicly or privately). I believe this publication will provoke you to be a better worshipper, because, no matter how good our worship and praise life is, there is always room at the top.

Some years ago, the Holy Spirit ministered to me that He had raised and empowered me not only to prepare great meals of worship and praise before God, but to help others understand the recipes for acceptable meals of worship.

In this book, I extensively explored what it means to be passionate. Our Lord Jesus was, and we cannot do less. God's presence is enormously powerful, and, in reading this book, you will further discover the importance of His presence in your life and the correct approach to connect with His presence. Our positioning is particularly important whenever we approach God's presence.

The Bible talks about the sacrifice of praise. But at what point does our worship become sacrificial? Remember that it is not difficult to praise God when all is bright and beautiful. But what happens when situations turn ugly? Sacrifice is one of the main ingredients of acceptable worship. It has a powerful voice that travels into the future. The first time "worship" appears in the Bible, it involves a case of absolute obedience and painful sacrifice. As you read this book, you will understand the difference between religious worship and spiritual worship.

Another mystery this book will unveil is the danger of considering people's perception and making public opinion to count whenever we worship God. I shared my personal experiences and some privileged revelations received from the Lord during encounters in the secret place. Passionate worship is a major requirement in accessing the secret place of the Most High. I examined the significance of the location and the power of self-denial. The secret of every great and genuine vessel in the hand of the Almighty is the power of the secret place.

You will further discover the manifold possibilities of our congregational or corporate worship. We often overlook some of these details I shared in this book, but I believe this will revolutionized our worship experience. I pointed out the roles of the music team, the media team and others in ensuring an impactful congregational worship, as well as the responsibilities of individual worshipers in the congregation.

Please place a copy of this book in the hand of every child of God you know - folks in the worship team, instrumentalists, the media team, church leaders, and so on. In doing so, we all shall be empowered by the Holy Spirit to take our worship life to a whole new dimension, where God will be truly glorified and the saints shall be edified!

CHAPTER ONE

IGNITING YOUR PASSION FOR GOD'S PRESENCE

The word "passion" is derived from the Greek word *pathos*, which signifies emotional affection, resulting from a strong attraction. In the Hebrew language, the word for passion translates as cleave. Therefore, the relationship between passion and cleaving is extraordinarily strong. A man cleaves to a woman in marriage, a tongue cleaves to the roof of the mouth.

To cleave is to love, to hold on to and unite with in a warm embrace. The English Dictionary also defines "passion" as a strong and barely controllable emotion. It is a feeling of intense enthusiasm towards, or a compelling desire for someone or something.

Therefore, passion involves putting energy into something than is required. It is more than mere excitement; it is a course of visible action from the human heart and soul. Some synonyms for passion are zeal, delight, fervency, desire, hunger, thirst and craving. Passion for God can thus be regarded as cleaving to God, resulting from a strong spiritual and emotional affection for Him.

Jesus was asked in Mark 12:28, **"Of all the commandments, which is the most important?"** And you can feel the intensity in His response, when He said, **"Love the Lord your God with all your heart and with all your soul and with all your mind and with all your strength"** (Mark 12:30). Now, that is a very passionate statement!

ATTRACTING GOD'S PRESENCE

The presence of the Lord in our lives is the best thing we could ever possess. The riches of this world cannot be compared with the glory that emanates from God's presence. God is everywhere but cannot be found everywhere. The manifest presence of God comes to those who seek Him - not for what they can get from Him or what He can provide, but for who He is. David said, **"As the deer pants for streams of water, so my soul pants for you, my God"** (Psalm 42:1).

Indeed, the Almighty God, in Jeremiah 29:13-14, says, **"You will seek me and find me when you seek me with all your heart. I will be found by you…"** The word "search" here connotes passion or desperation, a close pursuit of God with diligence. There is no discovery of the Lord and His delivering power for those who do not passionately pursue Him. His presence makes all the difference.

In Psalm 27:4, David cried out and said, "**One thing I ask from the Lord, this only do I seek: that I may dwell in the house of the Lord all the days of my life, to gaze on the beauty of the Lord and to seek him in his temple.**" The house of the Lord, in this context, is beyond the four walls of a physical building; David's desire was to be a constant carrier of God's presence. This is also why He pleads in Psalm 51:11 "**Do not cast me from your presence or take your Holy Spirit from me.**" He understood, he was nothing without God's presence.

It is noticeably clear throughout the scriptures that the power of God is resident in His presence. God cannot be present and His power absent. This means that we do not lack His power; what we lack is His presence. Divine presence carriers are Kingdom power brokers.

BLESSINGS OF GOD'S PRESENCE

1. The presence of God tears down obstacles and blows up strongholds of oppositions. Psalm 114:1-8 says: "**When Israel came out of Egypt, Jacob from a people of foreign tongue, Judah became God's sanctuary, Israel his dominion. The sea looked and fled, the Jordan turned back; the mountains leaped like rams, the hills like lambs. Why was it, sea, that you fled? Why, Jordan, did you turn back? Why, mountains, did you leap like rams, you hills, like lambs? Tremble, earth, at the presence of the LORD, at the presence of the God of Jacob, who turned the rock into a pool, the hard rock into springs of water."

The Bible also confirms that mountains melt and dematerialize at the almightiness of God. There is a solution to every issue of life - no matter how terrible or complicated it may seem. This means that matter ceases to matter at the instance of His presence. Isaiah 64:1 says, **"Oh that you would rend the heavens and come down that the mountains would tremble before you."**

2. The presence of God releases divine direction.

Exodus 13:20-21 reads: **"After leaving Sukkoth they camped at Etham on the edge of the desert. By day the LORD went ahead of them in a pillar of cloud to guide them on their way and by night in a pillar of fire to give them light, so that they could travel by day or night"**.

The voice of direction can be located or heard in the

presence of God. Remember, the face of God carries light and one major purpose of light is direction. Anywhere the will of God is, it is the best place to be. Whenever you feel confused about any matter, seek His presence and you will be guided aright. Psalm 89:15 assures, **"Blessed are those who have learned to acclaim you, who walk in the light of your presence, Lord."**

3. The presence of God creates miraculous openings.

John 20:19-26 narrates: **"On the evening of that first day of the week, when the disciples were together, with the doors locked for fear of the Jewish leaders, Jesus came and stood among them and said, "Peace be with you!" After he said this, he showed them his hands and side. The disciples were overjoyed when they saw the LORD. Again Jesus said, "Peace be with you! As the Father has sent me, I am sending you." And with that he breathed on them and said, "Receive the Holy Spirit. If you forgive anyone's sins, their sins are forgiven; if you do not forgive them, they are not forgiven." Now Thomas (also known as Didymus), one of the Twelve, was not with the disciples when Jesus came. So the other disciples told him, "We have seen the LORD!" But he said to them, "Unless I see the nail marks in** his hands and put my finger where the nails were, and put my hand into his side, I will not believe." A week later his disciples were in the house again, and Thomas was with them Though the doors were locked, Jesus came and stood among them and said, "Peace be with you!"

It is evident, from the above account, that if God is with you, you cannot be locked out or locked in. Anywhere God arrives becomes a passage - be it the Red Sea, River Jordan or within the four walls of any building. In Acts 16:26, as soon as the Spirit of God arrived at the prison where Paul and Silas had been chained down and locked up, **"there was such a violent earthquake that the foundations of the prison were shaken. At once all the prison doors flew open, and everyone's chains came loose.."**

4. The presence of God transmits virtue of healing and deliverance .

Acts 10:38 says, **"How God anointed Jesus of Nazareth with the Holy Spirit and power, and how he went around doing good and healing all who were under the power of the devil, because God was with him."** The presence of God is a supernatural river that flows with healing and deliverance virtue. Divine healing flows from His presence and burdens of all kinds are lifted. It is the natural atmosphere for the supernatural. Luke 6:19 says of Jesus Christ: "**And the people all tried to touch him, because power was coming from him and healing them all.**"

5. The presence of God activates supernatural supplies.

In John 2:1-4, we are told: "**On the third day a wedding took place at Cana in Galilee. Jesus' mother was there, and Jesus and his disciples had also been invited to the wedding. When the wine was gone, Jesus' mother said to him, "They have no more wine." Woman, why do you involve me?" Jesus replied. "My hour has not yet come.**"

We learn from the above experience that supply is guaranteed when God's presence is activated. Supply cannot run out when the Master is present because His personality magnetizes divine provision. Seun (my wife) and I have vivid and practical experiences concerning this. We have received help from strange, unbelievable and sometimes unknown quarters. In Luke 5:1-7, Peter received such a boat–sinking and net–breaking supply: "**One day as Jesus was standing by the Lake of Gennesaret, the people were crowding around him and listening to the word of God. He saw at the water's edge two boats, left there by the fishermen, who were washing their nets. He got into one of the boats, the one belonging to Simon, and asked** him to put out a little from shore. Then he sat down and taught the people from the boat. When he had finished speaking, he said to Simon, "Put out into deep water, and let down the nets for a catch." Simon answered, "Master, we've worked hard all night and haven't caught anything. But because you say so, I will let down the nets. When they had done so, they caught such a large number of fish that their nets began to break. So they signaled their partners in the other boat to come and help them, and they came and filled both boats so full that they began to sink."

Please understand that when the Master is present, you cannot be stranded because HE IS THE RIVER THAT NEVER RUNS DRY.

6. The presence of God imparts supernatural strength for victory in battles.

Numbers 23:21-23 says, **"No misfortune is seen in Jacob, no misery observed in Israel. The LORD their God is with them; the shout of the King is among them. God brought them out of Egypt; they have the strength of a wild ox. There is no divination against Jacob, no evil omens against Israel. It will now be said of Jacob and of Israel, 'See what God has done!"**

Beloved reader, I have come to realize that God's presence with a mortal man is the key to unbeatable strength in life. Divine presence carriers can never be weaklings in life. If God is with you, no battle or war can overcome you. The presence of God in your life equals the head of Goliath on the ground. David boldly declared in 1 Samuel 17:37, **"The LORD who rescued me from the paw of the lion and the paw of the bear will rescue me from the hand of this Philistine…"**

7. The presence of God gives rest and all-round peace.

Moses, in Exodus 13:14, exhorted the Israelites: **"In days to come, when your son asks you, 'What does this mean?' say to him, 'With a mighty hand the LORD brought us out of Egypt, out of the land of slavery."**

The presence of God is the sure cure for tension, stress, pressure and anxiety. It brings true joy and satisfaction. God's presence relieves depression and every other form of disorder. Remember that wherever God's presence is activated, strange spirits disappear. It is recorded in 1 Samuel 16:23 that **"Whenever the evil spirit landed on Saul, David would take up his lyre and play. Then relief would come to Saul; he would feel better, and the evil spirit would leave him."**

The seven points above and many more are enough reasons why we must passionately crave for God's presence.

ENTERING GOD'S PRESENCE

Having understood the value and power of God's presence, it is also pertinent to know how to enter His presence in a proper manner, so we can fully maximize the grace therein. When we speak of God's presence, we must understand that it has varying levels of manifestation. There are, at least, three of these to consider.

Firstly, God is omnipresent; His presence is everywhere all the time. This is the general manifestation of God's presence. Secondly, Jesus tells us in Matthew 18:20 that where two or three are gathered in His name, He is with them. This higher level of manifestation is apparently for believers only. Thirdly, we read in 2 Chronicles 5:13-14 of the account of the cloud of glory filling King Solomon's temple when the singers and instrumentalists lifted their praises to God. The presence of God became so tangible that even the priest could not perform their duties. This, again, is a much higher level of manifestation of the divine presence.

We still experience varying degrees of God's presence today, as we sometimes experience greater manifestations in our worship than the other. To come into God's presence (either as a congregation or as an individual) is to DESIRE to enter into a greater dimension of His glory and power. At such a moment, He is all that matters; He is all we see.

THE RIGHT APPROACH

In times of old, the Israelites approached God's presence mostly by songs of celebration and praise. We read in Psalm 95:2:

"**Let us come before him with thanksgiving and extol him with music and song.**"

Psalm 100:2-4 also says, "**Worship the Lord with gladness; come before him with joyful songs… Enter his gates with thanksgiving and his courts with praise.**"

We can also enter into God's presence with worship, as Psalm 96:8-9 exhorts: "**Ascribe to the Lord the glory due his name; bring an offering and come into his courts. Worship the Lord in the splendor of his holiness; tremble before him, all the earth.**" It is equally noteworthy that David, in Psalm 5:7, says: "**But I, by your great love, can come into your house; in reverence I bow down toward your holy temple.**"

While there is actually no universal formula for entering

into God's presence, it is important that we have our hearts fully engaged and rightly positioned to worship Him. This is why a corporate worship service may start either with high-tempo songs of joyful praise or slow songs of worship and adoration. Either approach is scriptural; so, worship leaders have the liberty to discern for each service how the Holy Spirit will lead us into His presence.

Chapter Two

INGREDIENTS OF PASSIONATE WORSHIP

One of the obvious reasons many folks approach God's presence and return without a definite encounter is that they are careless, and their passion is not involved in their worship. Passion is very costly. It involves a price; the giving of something that is very dear to us.

King David demonstrated this passion and zeal in 1 Chronicles 21:23-24, when he wanted to offer a sacrifice unto God on Araunah's threshing floor. "**Araunah said to David, "Take it! Let my lord the king do whatever pleases him. Look, I will give the oxen for the burnt offerings, the threshing sledges for the wood, and the wheat for the grain offering. I will give all this."** But King David replied to Araunah, "No, I insist on paying the full price. I will not take for the LORD what is yours, or sacrifice a burnt offering that costs me nothing."

One of my mentors once said, "If it doesn't mean anything to you, it may not mean so much to Heaven." This is very true. Therefore, let me show you some ingredients and necessities of an acceptable (individual or corporate) worship.

SACRIFICE

There is a direct relationship between sacrifice and passion. Any worship devoid of sacrifice and passion does not count before God. Hebrews 13:15 says **"Through Jesus, therefore, let us continually offer to God a sacrifice of praise—the fruit of lips that openly profess his name."**

The idea here is that praise or worship is not always what we feel like offering to God. Sometimes, if it must happen, it requires a selfless sacrifice on our part. We all love those moments when we feel like offering praise or worship to the Lord; but sometimes it is the last thing we want to do. Yet, God is worthy of our praise, even when our soul is disengaged or downcast. This is when it becomes real SACRIFICE.

We must train our spirit, mind and body to actively engage in praising God. I have realized that the best time to engage in passionate worship or praise is when things are not falling in place as expected. For example, when there is not enough money to pay the required bills; when your child is sick and you are so worried; when you have just received a negative medical report concerning your health; when the devil seems to be attacking your relationship; when disappointment from friends and trusted allies happens; and when there is an obvious delay in the fulfillment of a divine promise and it seems God doesn't really care. Beloved, these are the best seasons to engage in sacrificial worship and aggressive praise. We must shift the focus away from our circumstances and focus on God, for who He is.

YIELD CONTROL

The first place the word "worship" appears in the Bible is Genesis 22:5 and it is used synonymously as sacrifice. Abraham said to his servants, **"Stay here with the donkey while I and the boy go over there. We will worship and then we will come back to you."** The implication is that, beyond the congregational worship, God also expects us to present our entire lives as a sacrifice unto him. He wants our "Isaac" (what we hold so dear) on the altar of sacrifice. He wants to prove us, to ensure He takes the priority in our lives, because He is a jealous God (Exodus 20:5).

God expects us to yield control and serve Him with everything we have. He also expects us to base our decisions on His counsel and not on worldly wisdom.

He desires that we become His hands and feet in this lost and hurting world and place the need of others before ours. The beautiful thing is that, when we passionately seek to become a living sacrifice, we not only engage in true worship, but we find a life deeper, richer and more fulfilling than anything else we could imagine.

Being a living sacrifice is not easy and was never meant to be. When we strive to be a living sacrifice, we echo the words of Paul in Galatians 2:20, **"I have been crucified with Christ and I no longer live, but Christ lives in me. The life I now live in the body, I live by faith in the Son of God, who loved me and gave himself for me."**

FORGET NOT HIS BENEFITS

One of the main reasons some folks are not passionate about worshiping God is that they forget His benefits and their meditation is centered on what He is yet to do for them. Although they are physically present in God's presence - singing with their lips - their heart is far away from Him. Isaiah 29:13 describes such people this way: **"The Lord says: "These people come near to me with their mouth and honor me with their lips, but their hearts are far from me. Their worship of me is based on merely human rules they have been taught"."**

Again, for some individuals, the challenge is that they have come to see the mercies and blessings they enjoy from the Lord daily as their normal entitlements – and, consequently, they take it all for granted. This is why the psalmist spoke to himself thus: "**Praise the LORD, my soul, and forget not all his benefits—who forgives all your sins and heals all your diseases, who redeems your life from the pit and crowns you with love and compassion, who satisfies your desires with good things so that your youth is renewed like the eagle's**" (Psalms 103:2-5).

You also need to adopt the same attitude as the psalmist's. Never take the mercies of God as "normal", otherwise, you would not be able to worship Him passionately.

ATTITUDE OF GRATITUDE

We are often like the nine lepers in Luke 17, who received divine healing but refused to acknowledge the Healer. Here is the instructive narration: "**Now on his way to Jerusalem, Jesus traveled along the border between Samaria and Galilee. As he was going into a village, ten men who had leprosy met him. They stood at a distance and called out in a loud voice, "Jesus, Master, have pity on us!" When he saw them, he said, "Go, show yourselves to the priests." And as they went, they were cleansed. One of them, when he saw he was healed, came back, praising God in a loud voice. He threw himself at Jesus' feet and thanked him—and he was a Samaritan. Jesus asked, "Were not all ten cleansed? Where are the other nine? Has no one returned to give praise to God except this foreigner?" Then he said to him, "Rise and go; your faith has made you well." (Luke 17:11-19).

Jesus' emotional response to the ingratitude of the nine lepers gives us a glimpse into the heart of God. Jesus was disappointed that only one person cared enough to express his gratitude. This clearly shows that, sometimes, when we (believers) get what we want, we do not remember to show gratitude.

There are some salient truths to note about gratitude.

1. **Gratitude makes God happy.** 2 Chronicles 5:13-14 says, "The trumpeters and musicians joined in unison to give praise and thanks to the Lord. Accompanied by trumpets, cymbals and other instruments, the singers raised their voices in praise to the Lord and sang: "He is good; his love endures forever." Then the temple of the Lord was filled with the cloud, and the priests could not perform their service because of the cloud, for the glory of the Lord filled the temple of God." As the people wholeheartedly expressed

their gratitude to God, His glory came down mightily upon the temple and upon the worshipers – a clear indication that God was pleased with their action.

2. **Gratitude entails refusal to complain at all cost.** Complaining and grumbling are the biggest barriers to gratitude. We need to learn to caution ourselves when we are tempted to complain. Numbers 11:1 says the Israelites "**complained about their hardships**" and when God heard it, "**his anger was aroused**". We must avoid complaining, just as we would avoid a plague, because God hates it. The most important steps in developing inner peace is to quit complaining.

3. **Gratitude involves making a personal choice to rejoice.** It may be very difficult to be thankful at certain moments but we need to make a personal decision that we will remain grateful, even when we don't feel like it because things are hard. Apostle Paul wrote these words from prison, "**Rejoice in the Lord always. I will say** it **again: Rejoice!**" (Philippians 4:4). Notice the emphasis on "rejoice". Paul made a personal choice to be grateful, despite his circumstances. He was going to be thankful anyway. We must decide from now on to be thanksgiving addicts.

4. **Gratitude is a daily habit to be cultivated.** In order to remain a thankful people, it must become a habit. We need to discipline ourselves to find something each day to be thankful to God for. In Daniel 6, we read that Daniel got down on his knees three times every day, praying and giving thanks to God. We often think we are good if we give thanks once a day. But I want to challenge you to begin a regular routine of finding reasons every day to thank God. No matter how bad or ugly your situation may seem, you must learn to search out the positive aspect of it and give thanks to God. Count your blessings, not your losses!

5. **Be a deep thinker.** An African proverb says, "Only a deep thinker can effectively show gratitude." It is true. Please do not be bothered by the answer you are yet to receive; instead be thankful for where you are now because, whatever you are going through now is a shadow of what the devil actually planned for you. God is worthy of our appreciation; and appreciation of God is an application for more of His goodness.

BREAK THE ALABASTER BOX (VALUE YOUR RELATIONSHIP WITH HIM MORE THAN YOUR REPUTATION)

Another obvious reason many people cannot worship God passionately and go all out for Him (either publicly or privately) is because they are excessively concerned about their reputation. If you must truly express your passion for God, you must care less about public opinion and sometimes accept to look like a fool to many people in this world.

You rob yourself of righteous passion if you are too concerned about the perception of other people. It is a fact that your passion will be convicting to passionless people. Some may even hate you for this (I know from personal experience). But if you must give it all to Christ, you must sometimes get comfortable with making other people uncomfortable when they see your burning passion for Christ. It will unsettle some people, even fellow Christians, when they see how "reckless" you are in your worship and service. They will talk about you - how "immature" and "misguided" your actions are. They will sometimes try to convince you to slow down. But, please, do not give up your passion for the Kingdom.

In Luke 7:36-50 and John 12:1-7, Jesus defended Mary and her lavish gift. Surely, Mary knew she might be perceived to be a fool when she "wasted" a whole year's wages worth of fragrance on the feet of Jesus. But she had a burning passion for the Lord (as also evident in Luke 10:40-42), and she did not fear the way she would be perceived by people. She came to Jesus' presence weeping. Whatever was going on in her heart was deep; her tears signified her wholehearted repentance, affection and gratefulness. It was a sincere and unscripted worship. She kissed Jesus' feet and wiped them with her hair. She broke open the alabaster box of expensive fragrance and lavished it on His feet in reverent worship.

This is an authentic way to express worship because the Greek word for worship is *proskuneo*, which means to kiss the hand; or to do reference or homage by kissing the hand and bowing one's head in adoration. Thus, instead of being condemned by Jesus, as others were doing, it was a special affirmation and commendation that Mary got. **"Leave her alone,"** Jesus replied. **"It was intended that she should save this perfume for the day of my burial. You will always have the poor among you, but you will not always have me"** (John 12:7-8).

Indeed, passionate worship can never go unnoticed. It attracts attention because it is extravagant in nature, as demonstrated by this woman with the alabaster box of expensive fragrance.

RECKLESS ABANDON

One of my biblical role models is King David. In 2

Samuel 6:16-23, the Scripture records that he praised God with uncommon and unconventional passion. His wife, Michal (King Saul's daughter) despised him, thinking that a king shouldn't behave in such an undignified manner in the presence of a whole nation. Unfortunately and unknown to her, she was indirectly despising the Lord. And the consequence was truly tragic.

Here's what happened: "**As the ark of the LORD was entering the City of David, Michal daughter of Saul watched from a window. And when she saw King David leaping and dancing before the LORD, she despised him in her heart. They brought the ark of the LORD and set it in its place inside the tent that David had pitched for it, and David sacrificed burnt offerings and fellowship offerings before the LORD. After he had finished sacrificing the burnt offerings and fellowship offerings, he blessed the people in the name of the LORD Almighty. Then he gave a loaf of bread, a cake of dates and a cake of raisins to each person in the whole crowd of Israelites, both men and women. And all the people went to their homes. When David returned home to bless his household, Michal daughter of Saul came out to meet him and said, "How the king of Israel has distinguished himself today, going around half-naked in full view of the slave** girls of his servants as any vulgar fellow would!" David said to Michal, "It was before the LORD, who chose me rather than your father or anyone from his house when he appointed me ruler over the LORD's people Israel—I will celebrate before the LORD. I will become even more undignified than this, and I will be humiliated in my own eyes. But by these slave girls you spoke of, I will be held in honor." And Michal daughter of Saul had no children to the day of her death (2 Samuel 6:16-23).

Michal's experience carries a critical warning: If we become critical of genuine acts of worship, we could hazard spiritual barrenness, or even worse. Therefore, whosoever despises a passionate worshiper does so at his or her own risk!

The story of the woman with the alabaster box, which we considered previously, also exemplifies the "reckless abandon" ingredient of passionate worship. Perfumes (in those days) were often transported in alabaster vessels. Alabaster is a soft stone that looks like marble. It was a common material in those days. Therefore, the alabaster box was not really the reason for the value placed on Mary's act of worship but the expensive fragrance that the box contained. Yet, Mary broke the box; her passion was so strong that she did not hold anything back from the Lord Jesus. She was not going to save some of the perfume for a later date. *She wanted to get every drop of the perfume out of that bottle and give it to Jesus.* Likewise, when it comes to worshiping Jesus, it is expected that we would hold nothing back, for us to get the attention of the Master. Every part of us (spirit, soul and body) must be involved.

These are the days God is looking for men and women who will "ruin" their reputation, dignity, resources, and social status for the sake of Jesus. And you can be very sure that if you choose to be one of them, He will defend you at all times. Just love God passionately and show it. He will use your passion for His glory!

Chapter Three

WORSHIPING IN SPIRIT AND IN TRUTH

So, what exactly is worship?

It may be a bit difficult to give a "perfect" or an all-encompassing definition of worship because worship is a matter of the heart. It is spontaneous, infinite and as deep as the heart of God and those of his genuine worshipers.

Many equate worship with singing, but worship cannot be limited to songs. Singing is just one of the means of expressing our worship. Worship is a complete response to God, the focus of our worship. Worship is a lifestyle of giving to God the sacrifice He demands – our total selves (Romans 12:1).

An act of worship is our genuine response to the Father's love. Living should be constant worshiping, since worship may be said to provide metabolism for the spiritual life. Worship is our heartfelt expression of love, adoration and praise to God with an attitude of acknowledgement of His supremacy and lordship.

Worship can only be genuinely done by a redeemed soul, gratefully responding in reverence, honor and devotion to the revelation of God's person, expressed in the redemptive work of Jesus Christ. It is the ability to magnify God with our whole being – spirit, soul and body.

The act of passionate worship is pouring out our inner selves upon the Lord Jesus Christ in affectionate devotion. It is fundamentally God's Spirit within us connecting with the Spirit of the Godhead, whereby we answer, "Abba Father" - the deep calling to the deep (Psalm 42:7). Worship is extravagant love and absolute obedience to God.

TEST OF WORSHIP

Worship acknowledges the lordship of Jesus Christ in the face of life-shattering circumstances. Worship is not what we do only when the going gets good. Beloved, please remember that the true test of worship is not when we gather on Sunday morning with God's people - it is very easy to worship at such a moment. The real test begins on Monday morning when you return to the workplace or marketplace to mingle with the "uncircumcised Philistines".

The real test of worship happens when things are falling apart. I will illustrate this with two examples – one from the Scripture and the other from personal experience. Consider the experience of Job. The Scripture records that a crushing combination of calamities befell Job in one day. He lost his abundant livestock (his livelihood), his servants and all of his children in one day. Surprisingly, however, his response was extraordinary: "**Job got up and tore his robe and shaved his head. Then he fell to the ground in worship**" (Job 1:20). The test of worship occurs when our pain level hits the ceiling. And we have no idea what is happening to us.

In 2010, my wife was pregnant with beautiful twin girls and forcefully delivered them after six months, due to some complications. One of the babies died that same day and it was very painful indeed. I cried bitterly. We took the second baby home, christened and cared for her, until she became sick after two months, and we practically moved to the hospital. We spent all we had, but she died after four weeks.

However, although we had sympathizers taking their turns to pay us visits as expected, the following Sunday, my wife and I still wore our best clothes and went to church excitedly to lead worship – despite our pain and anguish. To God be the glory, as His presence came down mightily. After the service was over, a 70-year-old man said to me, "Daniel, what manner of faith is this? I have been young and now I am old, but I have not seen this kind of faith."

Shortly after, the Lord restored ALL our losses.

SPIRIT-LED WORSHIP

Only by the Spirit of God can we experience real worship and intimacy with God, as the Holy Spirit empowers us to connect with Him. In Romans 11:36, Paul explains that **"For from him and through him and for him are all things. To him be the glory forever! Amen."**

God created, designed and initiated worship. Also, our worship is lifted to Him who sits upon the throne. This means that true worship starts with God and ends with Him. In corporate worship gathering, we must acknowledge that the Holy Spirit is our Worship Leader. The role of the lead worshiper, therefore, is to follow the promptings of the Worship Leader. While it is expected of a lead worshiper to bring a set list, **a worship session cannot be successful if we merely follow our set list; it is successful only if we follow the spirit.**

A lead worshiper must follow the Holy Spirit, just as the Israelites followed the cloud of God's glory in the wilderness (Numbers 9:15-23). When the cloud moved, they moved, and when the cloud stayed, they pitched their tents. With every song we sing, the lead worshiper must seek to discern how long the Spirit is resting on that song, and they should not move on, it until "the cloud moves forward".

Following the leading of the Spirit is far more refreshing than following our order of service religiously.

GREATEST REVELATION ON WORSHIP

Jesus gave the greatest revelation on worship to a stranger – a Samaritan woman - when He said, "**God is Spirit, and his worshipers must worship in the Spirit and in truth**" (John 4:24). Let's take a deeper look at that statement. Jesus had come to the town of Sychar, an outskirt of Samaria, and was resting beside a well, while His disciples had gone to buy food. A Samaritan woman from town had come to draw water at the well, and Jesus had asked her for a drink. In the course of their conversation, Jesus made some supernatural observations about her life and it immediately became clear that she was in the presence of a prophet. Trying to change the subject of discussion and build a wall of defense around herself, she put forward an accusatory statement, "**Our ancestors worshiped on this mountain, but you Jews claim that the place where we must worship is in Jerusalem.**" (John 4:20).

Regardless of the motive with which the Samaritan

woman made the above statement, one thing was clear to the Lord – she needed to know what the right worship of God was and where to carry it out. Incidentally, this has remained a global human heart cry till today. This is why visitors visit our churches; because their hearts long to connect with God. Therefore, the Lord's house is first and foremost a house of prayer and worship. Every worship service must become a prayer meeting, so as to allow the people to connect with God. *And the best way a worship team can help the people to connect with God is by connecting to God themselves.* When observers realize that the team's connection to God is real, they will find courage to dive in and worship.

Jesus looked past the sins of the Samaritan woman and saw her yearnings and the hunger of her heart. He told her literally, **"Woman…believe me, a time is coming when you will worship the Father neither on this mountain nor in Jerusalem. You Samaritans worship what you do not know; we worship what we do know, for salvation is from the Jews. Yet a time is coming and has now come when the true worshipers will worship the Father in the Spirit and in truth, for they are the kind of worshipers the Father seeks. God is spirit, and his worshipers must worship in the Spirit and in truth"** (John 4:21-24).

The good news is that the Father is still seeking to connect with people today. He is not seeking for just worship; the scriptures confirm that He is seeking for worshipers. But the kind of worshipers He is seeking are not those who merely parade the outward forms, but those who possess inner sincerity and wholehearted affection. He wants the heart – all of it.

WORSHIP IN SPIRIT

True worship must be "in spirit". This means that worship is no longer confined to geographical locations or physical structures; rather worship can now take place within the "new temple" – the hearts of the people. 1 Corinthians 3:16 says, **"Don't you know that you yourselves are God's temple and that God's Spirit dwells in your midst?"** Believers now worship the Father at any time and at any place in the world.

Also, worship in spirit means that worship is no longer a function of rites or ceremonies but proceeding directly from the human spirit. Our spirit is the core of who we are. It is the center of our emotions and volitions. We also know that God is a spiritual being, therefore our spirit must connect to Him if we really want to worship Him. Under the old covenant, worship was a series of outward ceremonies and rites that did not necessarily involve the hearts of the participants. In Isaiah 29:13, the Scripture notes, "**The Lord says: "These people come near to me with their mouth and honor me with their lips, but their hearts are far from me. Their worship of me is based on merely human rules they have been taught"**.

But thanks to Jesus for inaugurating a new and better covenant in which worship is no longer merely the mouthing of empty clichés but, rather, the sincere expression of a pure heart.

WORSHIP IN TRUTH

Worship in truth means worshiping God based on accurate revelation and truth about who He is and what He does. Jesus distinguished between ignorant worship ("you worship what you do not know"), and inspired worship ("we know what we worship"). Additionally, the implication of Christ's declaration of the need to worship in truth is that worship that involves only the spirit is not enough. The more we focus our mind on the object of our worship, the Almighty God, the more meaningful our worship becomes.

Also, worship must happen through Jesus Christ, who is the Truth. In John 14:6, "**Jesus answered, "I am the way and the truth and the life. No one comes to the Father except through me."** When we worship in truth, we do not worship empty philosophies that come from the world's way of thinking; instead, we focus on the message of the Truth.

For us to worship in truth, we must know the Truth (Jesus Christ), and accept Him into our lives. Even when we think our relationship with God hasn't been impressive, He still wants us to draw near and be honest about it. To worship in truth does not mean we must be perfect, it just means we are not hiding or holding anything back from the Lord.

Worshipping in spirit without truth leads to a shallow and merely emotional experience that could be compared to an exaggerated exercise. Thus, as soon as the emotion is over and the fervor cools, the worship ends. On the other hand, worshipping in truth without spirit can result in a dry, passionless, and joyless experience. The combination of both aspects of true worship (in spirit and in truth) results in joyous appreciation of God, informed by the scriptures. The more we encounter God, the more we want to know Him; and the deeper our experience, the more our God is glorified.

SPIRITUAL WORSHIP VS RELIGIOUS WORSHIP

Spiritual worship is the worship of God done in the spirit and by the help of the Holy Spirit, while religious or carnal worship is the form of worship done as a routine. When worship becomes meaningless or done in the flesh, it is carnal and religious.

God is looking for spiritual worshipers and those who love to do it spontaneously. Religious worship may sound so sonorous and great, and the congregants may clap and be excited but it leaves them the same way. Spiritual worship, on the other hand, blesses and impacts lives, because it is born of the Spirit (John 3:6). Therefore, if our worship would be spiritual, the music team and worship leaders must devote time to pray more in the language of the Holy Spirit.

OUR RESPONSIBILITIES

When we attend a corporate worship service, we want to get as much as we can out of it. Although it appears that the responsibility to worship lies solely on the instrumentalists and the worship team, that is not true. 1 Peter 2:9 says of all believers: **"But you are a chosen people, a royal priesthood, a holy nation, God's special possession, that you may declare the praises of him who called you out of darkness into his wonderful light."** This means that all of us in the congregation are to minister to the Lord in worship.

The responsibility to bless the Lord does not rest only on pastors or the worship team but upon everyone in the meeting. Each of us has the responsibility to prepare our hearts for worship. We do this by spending time in prayer and in the word throughout the week. A prayerless Christian can never be a good worshiper. You can begin to pray and sing in your car on your way to the church to engage your spirit in worship.

Another way to prepare for worship is to deal with any known sin before we come into God's presence. Sin can hinder our freedom and confidence to approach God's presence. David said (after he had committed adultery with Bathsheba) in Psalm 51:3: "**My sin is always before me.**" The accuser of the brethren will always flash our past, especially unconfessed and unrepented sins, before us. This is why we must settle with the Lord before we approach His presence to worship.

Another good way to prepare is to brighten our countenance. We usually want to look good and joyful when we are invited to appear before an important personality. We groom ourselves, do good make up, and look radiant. The same way, when we appear before the Lord, we must put on a garment of praise, instead of the spirit of heaviness. Isaiah 61:3 says "**To console those who mourn in Zion, To give them beauty for ashes, The oil of joy for mourning, The garment of praise for the spirit of heaviness; That they may be called trees of righteousness, The planting of the Lord, that He may be glorified.**" (NKJV)

As we conclude this chapter, remember that God is

Passionate Worship

tired of lip singers and casual worshipers. He longs for those who will worship Him passionately, in spirit and in truth. I encourage you therefore to take your worship of Him to the next level.

CHAPTER FOUR

PRINCIPLES OF UNDISTRACTED WORSHIP

In this chapter, we will examine some of the distractions we experience during worship and how to eliminate them, in order to fully enjoy the showers of blessings that come upon those who engage in focused worship.

The human mind is prone to drifting, especially when it comes to spiritual matters. Such matters include studying the scriptures, praying, as well as praising or worshiping our Maker. Distractions do not stay in the car when we enter the church on a Sunday morning or during any of our services; they go everywhere with us.

We usually arrive at the church to sincerely worship God with focus, but the burden of the week, the unresolved issues, the tensions, the kids, the anxiety of our upcoming schedules and the wandering of our thoughts - all of these and more drift our attention back and forth. Interestingly, some of the biggest distractions come from the human dynamics at the meeting. These bring thoughts like: "The lead worshiper must be having a bad day"; "what's the pastor doing? He doesn't seem to be worshiping at all"; "that was a bad chord on the piano"; "the song is dragging - the drummer needs to increase the tempo"; "it doesn't seem like anyone understands this song"; "why is the sister dressed this way today?" etc.

We often think of distractions in passive terms, blaming the social media or our devices for distracting us. But distractions may also be our active choice to briefly escape something demanding. Thankfully, we are not slaves to our distractions. Therefore let's be encouraged, knowing full well that distractions in worship can be conquered. David says in Psalm 34:1 *"I have decided to bless the Lord at all times"* (paraphrased). No matter what seems not to be working, we must always make up our mind to engage our heart to bless the Lord.

REMEDIES AGAINST DISTRACTIONS IN WORSHIP

1. Focus your heart on the holiness and majesty of God.

Let God's majesty be your soul's constant meditation. Thomas Brooks wrote, "Oh! Let your souls be greatly affected with the presence, purity, and majesty of that

God before whom you stand. A man would be afraid of playing with a feather, when he is speaking with a king… There is nothing that will contribute so much to the keeping out of vain thoughts, as to look upon God as an omniscient God, an omnipresent God, an omnipotent God, a God full of all glorious perfections, a God whose majesty, purity, and glory will not allow him to behold the least iniquity."

Meditating on the glory of the King of kings will help redirect our focus and concentration, each time our hearts drift away. Isaiah 66:1 says, **"This is what the Lord says: "Heaven is my throne, and the earth is my footstool. Where is the house you will build for me? Where will my resting place be?"** Our God is so great that He sits in heaven and yet stretches His feet upon the whole earth. What a mighty God we serve! He is the creator of all things.

I was once privileged to visit the palace of an emir (a king and ruler) in one of the northern states of Nigeria, West Africa. The moment we entered the palace, we could perceive the aura of grandeur around the king. I observed that everyone either stooped or sat on the royal mats on the floor. No one could stand. We were all on the floor, bowing to the majesty of an earthly king, whose breath was in his nostril.

Now, imagine the glory and majesty of the King of

all kings and the Lord of lords, Governor among the nations, Creator of the universe and Ruler of the world! I have trained my soul to a point that I believe that one can master the act of focused worship, even when the instrumentalist is not playing the right chord or the sound is distorted. I have come to realize that what matters most is for me to connect to God's grace and virtue through His presence. Indeed, after every service, I always ask myself, "Did I truly worship God today?"

2. Prepare your heart before each service.

Before each service begins, devote time and efforts to prepare and make up your mind to encounter God through worship and praise, knowing full well that this is one of the sessions in which God is drawn towards us. Remember, Psalm 22:3 says specifically, **"But thou art holy, O thou that inhabitest the praises of Israel."** (KJV) The worship and praise aspect of all the programs is what directly goes to God; every other aspect of the service (the prayers, the testimonies, the message, the giving, etc.), are all for our edification as a church.

As the service begins, cultivate the sense of urgency and purpose. The moment the water of God's presence is stirred through worship, just jump in without any hesitation. Thomas Brooks again said, *"He that runs looks at nothing but the goal. Though he meets passengers, or pass by palaces, he is in earnest and stops for nothing. It is he that walks at leisure who turns his eyes to every trifle and beckons on every object because he is not in haste."*

My preparation for the any service begins a day before, in order to fully encounter and maximize God's presence. Whenever I wake up on Sunday morning, I fill my soul and spirit with His presence by listening to worship music. As we drive off the parking lot, I train my household to position our mind by praying in the Holy Ghost, all the way to the church.

3. Overcome pride of the heart.

Pride is possibly our greatest hindrance to focused worship. Pride could have hindered the sinful woman with the alabaster box from worshiping Jesus; instead, she poured her entire life out to Him. Pride has ruined more worship services (and deprived many of their blessings) than all the forces of hell combined. Pride prefers conservative, low-key, ego preserving worship.

Sometimes, pride restrains us from lifting our voices in the congregation. Pride robs us of the joy of dancing, lifting our hands, bowing down or crying in His presence. Pride says things such as, "Well, that's not just my way of praising God." When worship and pride clash, they can't both flourish at the same time. Worship prefers simplicity, while pride values self-glorification. Worship eagerly humbles self, so God can be exalted.

In Psalm 108:1, David said, "**O God, my heart is fixed; I will sing and give praise, even with my glory.**" (KJV) By using the word "glory", he meant that he would praise God, even with the reputation and status he had gained as king of Israel. David was a very prestigious king, who enjoyed riches, honor, and influence. But when it was time to worship, the most decorated and prestigious king would conduct himself recklessly, as a commoner, in the presence of the King of kings. David would gather his glory and the splendor of all he had accumulated as king, go as low as he could and pour it all out before the Lord. Worship was an opportunity for him to lift God high by going low.

We should constantly do likewise. We can gather all the glory of our attainment and pour it all out to Jesus, at every opportunity we have to worship Him. We must cast all the glory and crowns at His feet. After all, all the glory comes from Him in the first place.

Peer pressure is a brother of pride. Therefore, we must eliminate it because it can also hinder our worship. This is the natural tendency to be concerned about how we appear in the eyes of others around us. The desire for the approval of others around us can hinder us from pouring out ourselves to Jesus in worship.

4. Avoid being a spectator.

Another hindrance we need to consciously avoid is the tendency to look around during a worship service - watching everything that is happening, and getting so distracted by service dynamics and rules - that we never actually worship. Usually, while half of the congregation is worshiping, the remaining other half is watching. Yet, in God's Kingdom, there is no ministry called the ministry of surveillance. WE ARE NOT CALLED TO PRESIDE, BUT TO PARTICIPATE.

Some corporate worship is too often likened to a sport, where the congregation watches while the platform worships. This is a typical worship concert and not a worship service. A concert is where everybody sits or stands to watch and enjoy the performances of a set of folks and thereafter clap or rise in ovation of the performance. But a worship service is different. Here, everybody is expected to actively participate in the worship, meditate on the lyrics of the songs, close their eyes or keep them open, raise their hands etc. And God alone takes all the pleasure and the glory.

It's important to note that the success of the worship team lies in genuinely worshiping God and bringing the entire congregation with them.

5. Labor to be filled more and more with His fullness.

When we approach the presence of God, we should strive to keep our minds stayed on Him. The more we meditate on things of eternal value, the more our attention is committed to Him and the mundane things will grow strangely dim in the light of His glory.

This is a conscious effort, which involves avoiding activities like constantly checking our phones, reading emails, or looking up credit score, while the worship service is ongoing; and, instead, paying attention and meditating on scriptures. Ephesians 3:19 says, "**And to know the love of Christ, which passeth knowledge, that ye might be filled with all the fulness of God.**" (KJV).

IMPORTANT CHECKS FOR THE WORSHIP TEAM

There are some distractions that may happen from the worship team and we must be conscious to eliminate them. These include:

1. **Lack of preparation.** Just as a professional musician will not go for a performance without rehearsals, how much more the worship team that bears the vessels of the Lord! A worship team must take

practice and rehearsals seriously. Good preparation prevents poor performance.

2. **Song selection**. Instead of struggling to maneuver around difficult notes or keeping up with an upbeat tempo, worship leaders should choose selections that all in the congregations can wrap their vocal cords around.

3. **Weak lyrical display**. Songs are a major means of praising and worshiping the Lord. Please we must remember that the worshipers cannot instantly connect to worship if the lyrics of the songs are not properly displayed. The media team must aptly work to ensure the lyrics of the songs are correctly projected without errors.

4. **Facial expression**. The facial expressions of our worship team must reflect the songs they sing at every moment. This greatly helps the congregation to truly connect to the songs by the help of the Holy Spirit. If a worship team is singing about "joy like a river" (for example), and their facial expression reflects sadness or indifference, this may be a major distraction to worship. We must be conscious to maintain positive and matching facial expressions.

5. **"Preachy" worship leaders**. While the Holy Spirit may lead the worship leaders to a prophetic moment from time to time, making it a routine can cause

distractions to an effective worship service. Too much talking may disrupt the worship more than facilitate it.

6. **Poor sound and video quality.** If worshipers are straining to hear the worship team, it may cause a great distraction to the worship service. Occasionally, we can experience this difficulty, but the technical team must strive to avoid it, to ensure a hitch–free worship service

In conclusion, David declared in Psalm 57:7 "**My heart is fixed…I will sing and give praise**" (KJV). It is very important we make up our mind to worship the Lord in any situation we find ourselves. We must not play lip service by mouthing the words of a song, while our hearts won't connect to it. This is similar to the incident in Ezekiel 14:1-3: "**Some of the elders of Israel came to me and sat down in front of me. Then the word of the Lord came to me: "Son of man, these men have set up idols in their hearts and put wicked stumbling blocks before their faces. Should I let them inquire of me at all?"**".

We must mean every word we say during worship and say what we mean. Playing lip service is hypocrisy.

Chapter Five

THE SECRET PLACE

This is a very sensitive chapter and I implore you to pay close attention because we shall be exploring the mystery of "the secret place" and how to access this most crucial place in Divinity through the instrument of worship. God is called the omnipresent God, which means that He is everywhere in His sovereignty. However, He does not meet with people everywhere.

The Bible provides a proof of God's omnipotence in Psalm 139:7-10: "**Where can I go from your Spirit? Where can I flee from your presence? If I go up to the heavens, you are there; if I make my bed in the depths, you are there. If I rise on the wings of the dawn, if I settle on the far side of the sea, even there your hand will guide me, your right hand will hold me fast.**"

Yet, as already stated, even though God is everywhere, He does not meet with us anywhere. When businessmen want to meet, they do not meet at the roadside to discuss important transactions; they meet in designated places to have such discussions.

During my days as a Students' Union leader, I met one of the senators representing my senatorial districts and I found favor before this famous and rare-to-meet politician. While planning for my wedding, he asked me to see him and to my amazement, his orderly beckoned to me among many other people thronging to see him. I was led into his inner bedroom and I saw the most distinguished Senator was in a most relaxed manner and attire. He sat me down on his bed and we talked freely. He eventually gave me a very generous parting gift.

Everything from God flows out of the secret place. Everything good and lasting; everything that survives the test of time is born in the secret place. This is the season for every hungry, desperate follower of Jesus Christ to seek Him in the secret place.

SIGNIFICANCE OF THE SECRET PLACE

The word *secret* here means *hidden, private*. The implication here is that this is something between our heart and God's. He is in the secret, hidden, private place and He is always waiting for us there. The world, as well as many Christians, cannot find the secret place because they are trying to relate to God with their minds, laboring intensively in the strength of their own efforts.

He cannot be found that way. God and the things of the Spirit are only revealed to those who worship Him (and pray) in Spirit and in truth (John 4:24).

The apostle Paul tells us something similar in 1 Corinthians 2:14, "**The person without the Spirit does not accept the things that come from the Spirit of God but considers them foolishness, and cannot understand them because they are discerned only through the Spirit.**" In other words, we can only discern spiritual things with our spirits. Those same things seem foolish to our natural minds. But the rewards will be seen (openly) in every area of our life as we spend time in the secret place!

The Scripture also confirms in Proverbs 25:2 that "**It is the glory of God to conceal a matter,**

But the glory of kings is to search out a matter." (NKJV) God is an omnipotent Being and He is known to conceal great and valuable matters, just as He has hidden many of our natural resources deep down in the ground, and thus requiring efforts from us to dig them out. Truth is, everything that is glorious is hidden. Therefore, the best of Divinity is accessible only in the secret place. It is the system of God's Kingdom for uncommon manifestations in the life of any man.

Again, we read in 1 Corinthians 2:10 that "**these are the things God has revealed to us by his Spirit. The**

Spirit searches all things, even the deep things of God." No matter how talented or gifted a vessel is, there are certain dimensions of grace that he or she will not be able to manifest without spending quality time in the secret place.

DWELLING IN THE SECRET PLACE

The word "dwell" means to live in a specified place or to reside there. Psalms 91:1 says, **"He that dwells in the secret place of the most high shall abide under the shadow of the almighty."** (NKJV) Another version says **"He who stays in the High God's presence."** The good news about this scripture is that it says "he that dwells" or "he that stays"; therefore, we understand that it could be anybody. We also understand that dwelling is an individual responsibility and not a corporate effort, for the most part.

The secret place is not necessarily a physical location (although it is possible to create a physical place or a meeting point, dedicated to fellowshipping with God). It is a spiritual state or posture a man must maintain for him to access where God is. If it is the secret place, God will always be found there.

The need for the secret place is very necessary because there are some dimensions of God and some instructions from God that He will not reveal to us in the corporate setting or during congregational meeting. God loves men who seek Him. David declared in Psalm 63:1, "**O God, You are my God; Early will I seek You; My soul thirsts for You; My flesh longs for You In a dry and thirsty land Where there is no water**" (NKJV) The Lord visited Jacob when he was alone because he (Jacob) had created an atmosphere that became a secret place for him. He wrestled with Divinity; his name was changed and he received power with God and favor with men. He called the place "Peniel", meaning that he met with God face to face and his life was preserved (Genesis 32:22-30).

BENEFITS OF SOLITUDE

As we examine the life of Jesus, who is the author and finisher of our faith, we realize that, during His earthly ministry, He OFTEN withdrew into solitude to pray. Luke 5:16 says, "**But Jesus often withdrew to lonely places and prayed.**" Jesus knew He needed to temporarily escape the press of the crowd and the multitude of needs to be alone with the Father, as often as possible. This was the secret of His strength - the intimacy with the Father!

When it has to do with redemption, God reaches out to man; but when it comes to intimacy and our walk with Him, He waits for us to show our interest. Man must make effort to reach Him. This is one of the exercises any Christian should not downplay. Every time an eagle desires to renew its strength, the amazing creature retreats to a high mountain, in a lonely place, for a time of renewal. The same thing is applicable to us as believers in Christ. In Isaiah 40:31, the prophet describes the exercise as "waiting on the Lord". He says, **"But those who wait on the Lord shall renew their strength; They shall mount up with wings like eagles, they shall run and not be weary, they shall walk and not faint."** (NKJV)

Again, it is noteworthy that until Jacob was left alone, he could not encounter Divinity. Genesis 32:24 says, " **So Jacob was left alone, and a man wrestled with him till daybreak."** Israel, as a wonderful nation, would not have been born, if Jacob had not withdrawn into the secret place. Joseph's journey to his destination of becoming a Prime Minister was a journey of loneliness. He had to be away from his family, after being forcefully sold out. And when he thought he had finally found a family in Potiphar's House, he was again relocated into the prison for another season of loneliness. It was those seasons of being alone that birthed the destiny of the renowned Prime Minister of Egypt.

David too was basically alone in the wilderness. We read in 1 Samuel 16:11 that when Prophet Samuel went to visit the household of Jesse, so he might anoint a king, as commanded by God, David was the only son that was missing in that meeting. He was alone in the bush, keeping the flock. Samuel, however, insisted that nothing would be done until David returned from the bush. The anointing located the young guy in his lonely season.

THE POWER OF SELF DENIAL

In Matthew 16:24, Jesus said unto His disciples, **"Whoever wants to be my disciple must deny themselves and take up their cross and follow me."** Some people usually interpret this to mean that since Jesus suffered so much on earth for the redemption of mankind, then He expects His followers to have same experience. This is incorrect. Jesus did not intend this statement as an invitation to pain; He meant it as an invitation to intimacy with Him.

Beloved reader, if you really want to be close to Jesus, the key is self-denial, taking up your cross and following Jesus. This is an invitation to the highest level of intimacy, but we often avoid it because we think the price tag is too high. What we have not understood though is the value of what we are buying. Self–denial is the price for the incredible delights of a loving and consistent communion with our Lord. This a huge secret of engaging and enjoying the sweet fellowship of the Holy Spirit. It awakens the flow of life and love in the secret place.

Please note that denying oneself is not the same as taking up one's cross. To take up the cross may, in one sense, mean to crucify the sinful passion of the flesh. The cross has to do with the death of the flesh, the carnal man. Self-denial however has to do with deliberate curtailing and forsaking of healthy passions and desires for the sake of pursuing Jesus harder. Below are some of the ways we can deny self:

- Cutting back on sleep time, to worship and pray in the spirit.
- Bypassing good entertainment.
- Fasting or reducing intake of good food.
- Declining social invitations/fellowship.
- Lessening time given to recreation/exercise.
- Taking a temporary break from marital intimacy.
- Spending less when you could afford more.

Please understand that none of the above activities is sinful. Practiced in moderation, they are gifts from God for us to enjoy a fulfilling and satisfying life. However, some believers want more that a just happy life; we want to press into the secret place. We desire to know Jesus more intimately. We aspire to achieve Kingdom quest. We desire to acquire eternal treasures. We long for a fresh outpouring of God's Spirit in this generation. So, we must press into the Kingdom with spiritual violence.

The more we deny ourselves, the more the scales fall from our eyes. We will begin to see the world for what it is. Without self-denial, we naturally get desensitized to the filth of the worldly systems that surround us. The world denies itself nothing. So, when we embrace self-denial, we are doing something contrary to the worldly system.

1 John 2:15-17 says, **"Do not love the world or anything in the world. If anyone loves the world, love for the Father is not in them. For everything in the world—the lust of the flesh, the lust of the eyes, and the pride of life—comes not from the Father but from the world. The world and its desires pass away, but whoever does the will of God lives forever."**

Self–denial demonstrates that we do not love the world or the things in the world. It was lack of food that finally brought the prodigal son to his senses. **"When he came to his senses, he said, 'How many of my father's hired servants have food to spare, and here I am starving to death!"** (Luke 15:17). In a similar way, genuine spiritual fasting is a powerful asset in helping us to re-orient again to true Kingdom value and realities.

UNHINDERED COMMUINCATION WITH GOD

One of the prime benefits of the secret place through self–denial is the way it empowers us to hear more clearly from God. Answers, guidance, direction, insight, revelation and many more blessings flow freely when self–denial is willingly embraced with grace in our hearts. Jesus connected the secret place intrinsically with self–denial. He said, **"When you fast, do not look sober as the hypocrites do, for they disfigure their faces to show others they are fasting. Truly I tell you, they have received their reward in full. But when you fast, put oil on your head and wash your face, so that it will not be obvious to others that you are fasting, but only to your Father, who is unseen; and your Father, who sees what is done in secret, will reward you."** (Matthew 6:16-18). Self-denial is practiced in secret. It is done quietly and exclusively, to seek God and to be seen by His eyes alone.

In conclusion, when your secret place requires revitalization, embrace the grace of self–denial!

Chapter Six

THE POWER OF CORPORATE WORSHIP

The act of worship plays a particularly important role in our corporate gatherings. In this chapter, we shall identify why we worship together and the potency of corporate worship in our worship services.

Apostle Paul declares in Colossians 3:15-16, "**Let the peace of Christ rule in your hearts, since as members of one body you were called to peace. And be thankful. [16] Let the message of Christ dwell among you richly as you teach and admonish one another with all wisdom through psalms, hymns, and songs from the Spirit, singing to God with gratitude in your hearts.**"

These verses make a clear statement that speaks of the power of unity in our worship. We see that while the worship of our hearts is directed to God, some of the psalms, hymns, and spiritual songs are directed to each other! Please make no mistake - they are all about God, but the beneficiaries of the songs in these examples are the fellow believers.

The church must determine the role of congregational worship and what it is meant to fulfil in our local assemblies. Some churches view corporate worship as part of the preliminaries – that is, those aspects of the service that lead up to the most important element. This "most important element", for some of our churches, is the preaching of the word; while for others, it is prayer time.

A minister of God once rightly declared that "when the purpose of a thing is not fully understood, abuse is inevitable." I remember that, some years ago, while an invited guest preacher delayed his arrival for a particular meeting, the host pastor got on the pulpit to say, "Please while we expect the arrival of the guest preacher, let the choir continue to sing."

What he meant was that, since there was nothing else to do but wait, the church could use corporate singing to fill in the time. This is not the correct notion of congregational worship. Thankfully, with time, God began to instruct us on how to correct that misconception. After much waiting on the Lord, we started a movement that birthed several non-denominational worship seminars and trainings for pastors, worship leaders, soloists, instrumentalists, choir members and others, in the city of Ibadan, Nigeria. We created awareness and teachings about the importance and power of corporate worship. This soon birthed a revival movement that brought about a positive turnaround. And, in no distant time, most of our congregation realized that corporate worship time is the most crucial moment in any service.

During any congregational worship, as the people sincerely connect with heaven - with the right motive and attitude - they experience open heavens. There are words of prophecy, healings and instructions, and the body of Christ is edified. Paul, in 1 Corinthians 14:26, admonished the Corinthians: **"What then shall we say, brothers and sisters? When you come together, each of you has a hymn, or a word of instruction, a revelation, a tongue or an interpretation. Everything must be done so that the church may be built up."**

In congregational worship, the cry of the worshipper is not "bless me, Lord", but "bless the Lord, oh my soul". By blessing the Lord, we automatically get blessed. However, we do not bless Him in order to be blessed in return; we are called to minister to Him without any selfish motive. Still, He is a loving father; therefore, we must cultivate the attitude of blessing Him with our whole heart, not only in our private worship but also in the corporate worship atmosphere.

Proverbs 11:25 says, "**He who waters will also be watered himself**". Guess what? The corporate dynamics of our congregational worship is a reflection of our private worship experiences. And I cannot overemphasize that, although people worship together in a corporate worship atmosphere, most times, God reaches out to them individually, according to the depth of their heart's connection with Him.

STIRRING OF THE WATERS

One of the points I like to stress to all congregational worshippers is the understanding of the mystery behind the stirring of the spiritual waters. The Bible, in John 5, tells the story of the helpless man at the healing pool called Bethesda, who when the water was being stirred, had no one to assist him to get into the pool. One amazing revelation here is found in verse 4: "**For an angel went down at a certain time into the pool and stirred up the water; then whoever stepped in first, after the stirring of the water, was made well of whatever disease he had.**"

The Holy Spirit spoke to my heart many years ago during one of my encounters with Him, that if only the spiritual eyes of corporate worshippers could be opened to see the presence of angelic beings stirring spiritual pools during an intense corporate worship atmosphere, they would dive into the river of the Spirit to receive their healings in His presence. Yes, many times we feel His presence during our worship meetings, and yet many still find it hard to connect with Him. And, as a result of this, they return from the meeting feeling indifferent or even worse, because they failed to connect with God's presence during the corporate worship session.

I know this may not always be the experience, especially where there had been no preparation on the part of the worship team to create the correct atmosphere to receive angelic visitations. But it is a possible experience in all our worship meetings, and I encourage us to crave this experience with the Spirit of God. I trust the Holy Spirit to shed more light on this revelation in the heart of every reader of the book.

THE RIVER OF THE SPIRIT

One of the symbols of the Holy Spirit in the Bible is the Rivers of Living Water. John 7:37-39 records: " **On the last and greatest day of the festival, Jesus stood and said in a loud voice, "Let anyone who is thirsty come to me and drink. Whoever believes in me, as Scripture has said, RIVERS OF LIVING WATER will flow from within them." By this he meant the Spirit, whom those who believed in him were later to receive…"**

The Holy Spirit flows like an unstoppable river. However, one major responsibility required of every believer, as shown in the above passage, is THIRST. Without correct hunger and thirst for God's presence, we are bound to operate at a low-level experience in a congregational worship atmosphere. I see too many worshippers feeling indifferent and at ease during congregational worship. David was not at ease in worship, and the Bible has it that he praised God passionately. He declared in Psalm 35:18 **"I will give you thanks in the great assembly; among the throngs I will praise you."** Remember, the Bible says **"Woe to you who are at ease in Zion"** (Amos 6:1, NKJV). Therefore, I encourage you to increase your thirst because our level of thirst will automatically determine our level of encounter in the place of corporate worship.

I recall a situation in which a sister physically began to strangely swim on a dry, tile floor without any physical river, during one our worship meetings. She did this for several hours and her clothes got all dirty. Thereafter, she was asked the reason for such a manifestation and she answered that she saw a river and she dived in to swim and genuinely enjoyed the experience. The good thing is that, from that time, her life took a different turn, and she was never the same person after the encounter.

Prophet Ezekiel says in Ezekiel 47:9, "**Swarms of living creatures will live wherever the river flows. There will be large numbers of fish, because this water flows there and makes the salt water fresh; so where the river flows everything will live.**". The River is so powerful and can fix anything wherever it flows. And I want us to believe that each time we gather in a congregational worship, the River of the Spirit is present to heal and refresh. But we have the responsibility to believe, connect and correctly channel the River. In Revelation 22:1-2, John on the Island of Patmos, wrote "**Then the angel showed me the river of the water of life, as clear as crystal, flowing from the throne of God and of the Lamb down the middle of the great street of the city. On each side of the river stood the tree of life…**"

PRESSING THROUGH THE CROWD

The corporate worship atmosphere is a crowded setting. Indeed, anywhere two, three or more are gathered is already a corporate worship setting. Yet, each individual is expected to press through in order to touch Jesus.

Let me re-emphasize that it takes intentionality, focus and determination to press through. The woman who pressed through in the scriptures was desperate and resilient and as she touched the hem of Jesus' garment,

Passionate Worship

she suddenly realized a new dimension of peace and joy in her life. It was her passionate pursuit of Jesus that caused her miracle to become manifested (Matthew 9:20–22).

Now, to the faithful and persistent worshipers who press their way through the realms of religious mediocrity and gain entrance to the Holy of Holies, God promises He will be there, waiting to transform our lives, just as He did for this woman. But remember that PASSION is a major requirement to press in and touch Jesus. Even if you have once touched the hem of Jesus' garment, I encourage you to go again and again to touch Jesus, because "just enough may not be enough".

Heaven is waiting to receive your passionate worship and praise more than ever. And as you make time to intentionally pour it all out at the Lord's feet, the aroma of His presence will fill your life and home, and you will begin to enjoy all of Him more than ever.

Chapter Seven

THE POTENT WEAPON OF WARFARE

God has given us (believers) several spiritual weapons, and the power in these weapons is enormous. These weapons include the name of Jesus, the blood of Jesus, the words of our testimonies and so forth. But I will be elaborating on the weapon of worship and praise and share some practical testimonies with you.

Apostle Paul declares in 2 Corinthians 10:4 that **"the weapons of our warfare are not carnal, but mighty through God to the pulling down of strong holds."** (KJV) No physical or fleshly weapon is potent when it comes to fighting an unseen adversary; it takes spiritual weapons to defeat spiritual enemies. Worship and praise is one mighty weapon that the enemies are afraid of.

Satan detests genuine worship and praise because he understands its powerful effects. The Bible makes it clear that Satan (Lucifer) was the most beautiful and powerful being ever created. He was the supreme archangel, just like Gabriel and Michael. Moreover, he was a matchless musician. Ezekiel 28:13 says, **"The workmanship of your timbrels and pipes Was prepared for you on the day you were created."** (NKJV)

Modern music history confirms that Satan has profound musical abilities. So, I do not think it is a coincidence that music artistes who promote immorality and all other forms of ungodliness often enjoy a supernatural rise. In Isaiah 14:12, the Bible describes Lucifer as the morning star and son of the dawn. What a wealth of glory he carried due to the position he was as the music leader in heaven! For this reason, Satan hates it whenever an intense worship or high praise is being offered to God, because it is usually irresistible to God and when He arises, He rides on the wings of our praise to execute judgment upon the enemies. Psalms 149:6-8 says, **"May the praise of God be in their mouths and a double-edged sword in their hands, to inflict vengeance on the nations and punishment on the peoples, to bind their kings with fetters, their nobles with shackles of iron."**

CERTAINTY OF VICTORY OVER OUR BATTLES

Beloved, please understand that as real as the battles that confronts us, so also is the reality of our victory.

We have divine assurance of victory over all spiritual, physical and psychological enemies like sorrow, depression, loneliness, trauma, sicknesses and diseases, crimes and violence, and so on. Corporate worship or praise remains a potent weapon of assault on the gates of hell. Private praise is equally combative.

Indeed, from the Scripture, praise can be seen as a militant activity - going all the way back to the Israelites' crossing of the Red Sea. The Egyptian army had just drowned in the rushing waters, and the people of God were safe on the other side. Miriam grabbed a tambourine and led the people in high praise: **"Sing to the Lord, For He has triumphed gloriously!**

The horse and its rider He has thrown into the sea" (Exodus 15:21, NKJV).

On that same occasion, Moses had previously led all Israelites to sing a triumphant song of victory to the Lord and celebrated with this declaration **"The Lord is a man of war; the Lord is His name"** (Exodus 15:3, NKJV). After seeing how God dealt with Pharaoh and his armies, they knew they had witnessed a great battle strategy in action.

The Lord also revealed Himself as a mighty warrior to Joshua. As Joshua was about to lead the Israelites across the Jordan River into Canaan, a man appeared unto him with a drawn sword. Joshua asked him, **"Are you for**

us or for our enemies?" "Neither," he replied, "but as commander of the army of the Lord I have now come"' (Joshua 5:13-14).

Furthermore, the Bible has some marvelous stories of God accomplishing great victory for His people in response to their praise. One of the foremost instances was in the days of King Jehoshaphat, when the Edomites arose to invade Judah. Alarmed, Jehoshaphat gathered all Judah to the temple to seek the Lord. In his prayers, he said "Our God, will you not judge them? For we have no power to face this vast army that is attacking us. WE DO NOT KNOW WHAT TO DO, but our eyes are on you." (2 Chronicles 20:12). In response, the Spirit of the Lord came upon a Levite named Jahaziel, a descendant of Asaph (the music director of King David). Jahaziel proclaimed, "Listen, King Jehoshaphat and all who live in Judah and Jerusalem! This is what the Lord says to you: 'Do not be afraid or discouraged because of this vast army. For the battle is not yours, but God's...You will not have to fight this battle. Take up your positions; stand firm and see the deliverance the Lord will give you, Judah and Jerusalem. Do not be afraid; do not be discouraged. Go out to face them tomorrow, and the Lord will be with you" (verses 15-17). With his faith strengthened, Jehoshaphat later stood and declared, ""**Listen to me, Judah and people of Jerusalem! Have faith in the Lord your God and** you will be upheld; have faith in his prophets and you will be successful'"" (verse 20).

One lesson I must stress here is this: **Praise is what to do, when we don't know what to do!** When the battles are raging and the threats from the adversary are ringing loudly, we should switch to praise. Imagine that Jehoshaphat had ignored the prophecy from Jahaziel. What would have happened to Judah? But thank God, he believed God's assurance that they did not need to fight, but just to watch and see the salvation of the Lord. I can imagine him saying, "Well, since that is the case, let us mobilize a national praise team." The Bible reveals that they marched on with high praise to face a great and highly weaponized army. All they had was thanksgiving to God for the victory they had not physically obtained. This was bold faith.

Another lesson here is that **faith is a necessity in order to realize the fulfilment of prophecy.** Jehoshaphat refused to doubt the prophecy. So, all they did was to offer praises to God who had promised and who was able to do exceedingly and abundantly far above what they could ever imagine. So, off they went to war with the choir singing and the army following. They praised the beauty of God's holiness saying, "**Give thanks to the Lord, for his love endures forever.**" (verse 21).

What happened next? "**As they began to sing and praise, the Lord set ambushes against the men** of Ammon and Moab and Mount Seir who were invading Judah, and they were defeated. The Ammonites and Moabites rose up against the men from Mount Seir **to destroy and annihilate them. After they finished slaughtering the men from Seir, they helped to destroy one another. When the men of Judah came to the place that overlooks the desert and looked toward the vast army, they saw only dead bodies lying on the ground; no one had escaped. So Jehoshaphat and his men went to carry off their plunder, and they found among them a great amount of equipment and clothing and also articles of value—more than they could take away. There was so much plunder that it took three days to collect it"** (2 Chronicles 20:22-25).

The real warriors in the experience above were not the soldiers, but the singers. The mystery here is that they did not even address their enemies; they focused on praising God, who had promised them victory. With their FAITH-FILLED PRAISE, they spurred God to act according to His wisdom and power. They were not telling God how to defeat their enemies, they were just praising Him, knowing full well that **"Faithful is he that calleth...who also will do it"** (1 Thessalonians 5:24, KJV).

Praise warfare does not have to tell God what to do. It praises Him for His wisdom and might, recognizing that He is capable of settling the problem in a way that best glorifies His name. Praise warfare does not focus on the battle or the enemy; it looks only to the solution – God! Daniel 11:32 assures, **"But the people that do know their God shall be strong, and do exploits."**

PRISON BREAK

Another famous example is found in Acts 16. Paul and Silas had been arrested in Philippi for preaching and delivering a demon-possessed girl. They were heavily flogged with rods and then thrown in the city jail. Not only were their bodies bleeding and swollen, but the chains were designed to add to their misery.

Beloved, what do you do when you are in physical pain or emotional trauma? Perhaps you are sick in your body or you are being abused, ridiculed, or maltreated at work or suffering from relationship abuse. Perhaps your kids are not doing well and turning against you. Whatever the situation or "prison" you may find yourself in, **the key to unlocking the chains and break free is intentional PRAISE.**

Unable to find a comfortable position, Paul and Silas began to lift their voices in praise and thanksgiving to God and they did not hold back. The Bible reveals that they sang so loudly that all the prisoners heard them. They advertised Jesus in their pains and afflictions.

Remember that, at this point, they were not asking for deliverance or calling fire down on the city council that maltreated them; neither did they curse the jailer. They simply praised God for His greatness and power to save. They had no idea what was going to happen. Then… **"suddenly there was such a violent earthquake that the foundations of the prison were shaken. At once all the prison doors flew open, and everyone's chains came loose."** (Acts 16:26). The story ends with the same jailer who had inflicted pain on them, turning around to kneel before them in deep remorse, and asking what he must do to be saved. He nursed their wounds and served them a sumptuous meal. The lesson here is, when we praise God in our chains and pains, God will step in and turn around the situation for our testimonies.

THE SHOUTING SIDE IS THE WINNING SIDE

The shout of praise was instrumental in bringing profound victory in many biblical stories. For example, the Israelites used the shout of praise to overcome the city of Jericho. For six days, they marched around the city each morning. On the seventh day, they rose early in the morning to march round the city seven times. Here's the battle plan for Joshua. After the seventh time around the city, the trumpeters were to sound and then the people were to lift their voices.

And so it happened that **"when the trumpets sounded, the army shouted, and at the sound of the trumpet, when the men gave a loud shout, the wall collapsed; so everyone charged straight in, and they took the city."** (Joshua 6:20). Was it really that shout that caused Jericho walls to collapse? No, God acted on their behalf. The host of heaven came down to take dawn the walls as they obeyed divine instructions.

I love quiet moments when we stand in awe before the Lord but there are times when silence is not appropriate. There comes a time to really shout. It is a sad day when shouting is departed from the tabernacle. The Bible confirms that **"The voice of rejoicing and salvation is in the tabernacles of the righteous: the right hand of the Lord doeth valiantly"** (Psalm 118:15).

TESTIMONIES FROM MARATHON WORSHIP/ HIGH PRAISE SHOUT

In 2014, the Lord ministered to us and instructed us to raise an annual altar of 48 Hours Marathon Worship in Ibadan, Nigeria. In obedience to this instruction, we mobilized worshipers across various denominations to take their turn as we sang praises to God. We had several testimonies, ranging from miraculous healings to divine lifting and promotions. We heard of supernatural favors and divine blessings, as well as miracle conceptions,

Passionate Worship

after having waited on the Lord for several years. But there was a year that one of the guest ministers just instructed us to shout a great shout. And behold as we lifted our voices to shout, the power of the Holy Spirit hit everyone in the arena - chains began to lose, the oppressed began to scream, "I am free!" There was deliverance from marine spirits and lots more.

Indeed, it was as if the hosts of heaven were waiting for that shout of victory, to invade the arena. The shout brought down an experience that was noised abroad due to the testimonies that followed it.

When we moved to the United States to continue the ministerial assignments, we continued the marathon worship experience with 24 Hours Marathon Worship, as requested and permitted by our lead pastor in 2019. It was a glorious experience, greeted with diverse testimonies. In 2020, we decided to host a hybrid version of the marathon worship, due to COVID-19. It was an outdoor and online experience. One of the major testimonies we received read:

I am based in Ghana, Africa, and I have been diagnosed of liver problem due to the life I lived in school. I have also been admitted at the hospital in the last six months, while on dialysis. I was on the bed yesterday, scrolling through my phone, when I stumbled on an online marathon worship session on Facebook. I clicked to watch, since I could not go to church. I saw one pastor sitting on the altar and was praying. Thereafter, he introduced a pastor from Nigeria to lead worship (Pastor Cylars Omoloye).

I followed this session because I love this man's energy and the way he sang. I started singing unconsciously and moving my body. It was a miracle doing that because I had not been able to move that way for a long time. I kept singing and at a point I began to shout "I AM HEALED!" The doctors rushed into my room to check what was wrong. They were amazed to see the excitement on my face, and my body moving in such a manner as they had not seen before. I continued the praise and suddenly I slept off. Then I had a dream that a pastor and a doctor came to my bed to perform a surgery on me. I woke up in the evening. Beloved, I woke feeling extraordinarily strong and not feeling pain. My body system has changed. I believe I am healed!!!!

Indeed, the shouting side is the winning side. It does not matter what you are going through. Remember, PRAISE IS WHAT TO DO, WHEN WE DON'T UNDERSTAND WHAT TO DO. You too will testify of the miracle and deliverance power that is in the weapon of praise.

Welcome to your new season!

ABOUT THE AUTHOR

'Kayode Fagbe Daniels is the Resident Pastor and Music Director of the RCCG, Jesus House, in Antioch, California; and president of the Judah's Voice Ministries Int'l.

Pst. Kay, as fondly called, is a revivalist, burning with passion to see the advancement of God's kingdom. He is a lover of God and genuine worshiper of the living God. Due to his evangelistic calling, he has been an instrument in the re-awakening of several souls on different platforms.

Kay is a God-chaser, with a mandate to see the revival fire on the altar of worship and rebuild the broken altars of praise (Amos 9:11). He published a music magazine (Soul-Train Music) in 2003. He is a conference speaker and song writer, with grace to pray.

A linguistic graduate from the University of Nigeria, Nsukka (UNN), he once served as a bilingual Business Development Manager at a multinational organization, with proven track records.

Passionate Worship

He is happily married to Seun, an energetic lead-worshiper and they are both blessed with three generals

Connect with me on Social Media:

Facebook@ Kayode Fagbe - Daniels

Instagram@ kayodemcdaniels

www.ingramcontent.com/pod-product-compliance
Lightning Source LLC
LaVergne TN
LVHW051847080426
835512LV00018B/3125